Aradhana
(Adoration in Love)

Aradhana
(Adoration in Love)

K.K. Mohanty

BLACK EAGLE BOOKS
2021

BLACK EAGLE BOOKS

USA address:
7464 Wisdom Lane
Dublin, OH 43016

India address:
E/312, Trident Galaxy, Kalinga Nagar,
Bhubaneswar-751003, Odisha, India

E-mail: info@blackeaglebooks.org
Website: www.blackeaglebooks.org

First International Edition Published by
BLACK EAGLE BOOKS, 2021

ARADHANA
(Adoration in Love)
by K.K. Mohanty

Copyright © **K.K. Mohanty**

All rights reserved. No part of this publication may be reproduced, stored in a retrieval system, or transmitted, in any form or by any means, electronic, mechanical, photocopying, recording or otherwise without the prior permission of the publisher.

Cover Design: **Subarna Ghoshal**
Interior Design: Ezy's Publication

ISBN- 978-1-64560-209-5 (Paperback)
Library of Congress Control Number: 2021945700

Printed in the United States of America

For Lily
My Poetry of Life

A Word of Thanks

'God bless your pen' – that's how Dr P.G. Ramarao, eminent professor of English literature, blessed me after reading a few of these poems. I bow to him humbly.

Nidhi Sen and Himalika for reading the poems and making valuable suggestions.

Kenneth K. Mohanty who thought the inspiration could have been differently poeticized.

My FB friends – Rabindra Nath Sinha, Gauranga C. Raul, Narayan Chandra Das, Arun Patnaik, Mihir K. Sahoo, Abhas K. Boral, Nihar Roy, Anasuya Acharya, B.K. Mohanty, Narayan Raul, Chanda, Fulki, Tarun, B.N. Mohanty, and others who enjoyed some of these poems posted on Face Book.

A Submission

These poems are largely inspirational. The inspiration was a heart-winning woman whose name, unfortunately, I do not know. I did not meet her the way one meets a stranger. I guess she was a high school teacher and she came to say `hello' while I was returning after attending a school function. I was stuck by her beauty and her comeliness. She said a word or two, but before I retuned compliments she was off. Those who have read `Darling' – the translated version of poet Phani Mohanty's long odia poem `Priyatama' – might have noticed in my submission that while translating the poem I fell in love with an unknown woman. This unknown woman has come to stay in my heart as a perennial source of poetic inspiration. She has become my Aradhana - adoration in love. I love to call her Jina which means winner of hearts. Her name I will not know; she will always remain Jina to me…and, of course, my Aradhana.

Poetry offers strange possibilities. It is perhaps the most dependable medium to express dreams, create a world according to wild specifications, think weird thoughts and discover a channel to translate the whims into reality. In poetry one has an option to close the eyes to see better, or keep the eyes open and see nothing. Seeing nothing is an art that is acquired without any conscious effort. A good example of it is T.S. Eliot who saw women coming/going in the room talking of Michelangelo. Did Eliot see women coming; did he hear them talking? For him Michelangelo might have been the inspiration, but can Michelangelo get poetized if women do not talk about him. It was a startling revelation. An Eliot reader has no difficulty in seeing with closed eyes women who shone beautifully in the room which received scant sunlight. Hearing them talk is subtler art; beauty sings tunefully always. The nameless woman who touched my heart so intensely inspired me both by her physical charm and her musical voice, which I am yet to hear.

Frost's `Butterfly' may be another example. Robert Frost wrote `My Butterfly' when he was nineteen. He wrote it in one go in the kitchen room. He locked the door and all the time was working. Even as he wrote he had ``sensed in a way that something was happening. It was like cutting along a nerve.''

Frost got something there, and he knew it. ``That was like a blush. Never thought of that before. Poetry is like a cry…But it is like a blush…you can get something you didn't know you had.''

Can there be some commonality in Wordsworth's `Daffodils' and Frost's `Butterfly'. Daffodil, the flower, and butterfly the insect both beget poetic inspiration. This is suggestive: Anything, animate or inanimate, big or small may inspire a poet, and once inspired the poet sings of them as the very soul of his creativity. A poet helplessly made to follow his inspiration is the root factor in making poetry the most appealing art of literature. If the ``sweetest voice of love'' overwhelms a poet (Robert Southey), another poet

(P.B. Shelly) hears ``sweetest songs'' that ``tell of saddest thoughts'', and yet another poet (Lord Byron) thinks that sweeter than anything is ``passionate love if stands alone.'' Isn't sweetness a strange poetic inspiration? It touches all human emotions - anxiety, sadness, love et al. While walking on streets, looking through my window, walking casually in a park I always feel that the flowers, the greenery, the trees, the sky, the clouds – all this is created to fulfill God's mission to make man poetic so that His creation will have a real meaning beyond the physical. It may be said that it is Nature that provokes a scientist to search into its mysteries, and it inspires a poet to sing of the Nature that contains the Creator's greatness. I believe the poet is dear to God. And those who read and enjoy poems are God's assurance to a poet that he would be appreciated by those who see the Divine in the beautiful Creation.

A scientific discovery/invention begins from the lab and it reaches everyone even without their knowledge. That is the all-pervasiveness of science. But poetry is an art of consciousness; it can't touch all, it can't make all hear the esoteric call that comes from within. Not many are aware of their Inner call, not many have the faintest idea of some higher, subtler and mightier force residing in their Inner world waiting to communicate with them. In most cases the higher – that is in fact, the creative force – remains dormant in a man and dries up day by day. The reason man becomes mechanical in his approach to life is: Engrossed as he is in scientific gadgets, he finds no time to think of his finer creative constituents. True, scientific gadgets bring immeasurable material joy that's enough to keep man bound to it. 'Joy' is defined as 'Maya' in Indian philosophy. Maya – that is roughly translated as illusion – does not really clutch a man to stay glued to it; man gets automatically glued to Maya because he doesn't want to imagine that there can be something beyond physical comfort provided by Maya. Metaphysics may be an ingredient of Maya, but it is at the escape point. A reader of literature who loves literary comfort may have his wishes gratified from several sources; but once he comes to taste the nectar called poetry he would not have any need for any other literary comfort. He knows the taste is supremely sweet.

That is the reason the earliest world literature came in the form of poetry. The Ramayana, the Mahabharata, the Bhagabatam, the puranas and other such earliest texts provide a platform to sing before understanding the message. Those who read those epic poems may not hesitate to admit that more than their intrinsic worth they are popularly accepted and piously recited for their lyrical charm. It is difficult to gauge why exalted souls such as Balmiki and Vyasa thought it fit to narrate God's glory in poetic metres instead of stating it in plain prose. A reader or a listener may not have occasion to think about the form of puranic presentation; they are simply overwhelmed singing and hearing the Divine lila. Needless to say, poetry is natural to man's literary taste; a literary critic may get a convincing idea about this seeing an Indian farmer sing puranic lyrics while cultivating his field. Even the bullocks yoked to the ploughshare are said to be pulling the appliance most willingly when the farmer is in a poetic mood, singing ancient verses.

Poetry has been a sure source of delight and diversion to tired souls and happy folks. Centuries ago captivating tales of war and morals were told by learned people in poetic form. In Odisha, an eastern territory in India that is known for its literary excellence, Sarala Dasa, the poet of the masses, sang the episodes of the Mahabhrata in free verse that modern critics view with wonder. The same can be said about Geoffrey Chaucer and John Milton, whose poetic works enriched English literature and provided the masses a means to tell or hear stories in uneven verses. That was how poetry came to occupy the literary imagination worldwide. William Shakespeare was an excellent storyteller. He chose to present historic themes in theatre. All Shakespearean plays are a mixture of delightful dialogues and free flowing appetizing rhymes. Seeing Mark Antony addressing ``Friends, Romans and countrymen'' is perhaps one of the most stirring poetic presentations in world literature. It can be said, arguably, that that speech worked wonders because it was delivered rhythmically. Any other form of presentation would not have produced the desired effect. A more recent case is Lincoln's Gettysburg address. Historians see it as an ``unconscious prose-poem…(with) all the majestic beauty and profound roll of epic lines.'' A government ``of the people, for the people, by the people'' is an idea conceived in poetry. It has become a guiding principle of American democracy. In fact, poetry is an art of the Unconscious; it evolves with no conscious explanation. Poetry has the potential to teach people to reason and stir them to patriotism. It has equal potential to arouse people to love and passion and to a much higher sensibility called devotion. A political speech that stirs people to move in a body or agitate, risking their lives, is mostly poetic. Winston Churchill created an unprecedented impact on the world with his "blood, sweat, tear and toil" appeal. Didn't the call to fight on the beach and sand and open space arouse the world to stand by him because Churchill was issuing a poetic challenge to fight Nazism and Fascism that were so crude and far removed from poetic sensibility.

And then Netaji Subhas. When he asked for blood to win Independence he was transmitting a message of love to those who loved to be free. Jawaharlal Nehru also sang the same tune. Cast in a poetic mould his ``tryst with destiny'' remains as the last reference point of India's freedom struggle. It is astounding because Nehru's oration was poetical.

Inculcating poetic sensibility gives a different meaning to life. Can the pinching mundane realities around us be poetic? This may vary. But the eyes that see nature as benign, the elements as emotive, will automatically be charged with the different meaning of life. The Chilka is a fabulous lake on the Odisha coast. Every year thousands of nature lovers throng there to get a touch of the sea, hills, and the innumerable varieties of birds that delightfully crowd the blue expanse of the lake (actually a lagoon on the Bay of Bengal). Personalities such as Napoleon and Lincoln have always something new for a history scholar to say about them; similarly, the Chilka has always something new to offer to an empathetic heart. Literature on the alluring lake abounds. But seldom does the reader get to read anything on the Chilka that isn't poetry. Great Odia poets such as Radhanath Roy, Gopabandhu Das, Godavarish Mishra sang a lot about the lake, enriching Odia literature in a meaningful way. One wonders if Odia literature would not be poorer if Chilka is not poetized, and if Chilka would not be poorer if she is portrayed in any form other than poetry.

If there is an inherent tendency in man to appreciate and worship beauty it's because the Nature around us is beautiful. Then there's the physical charm of the created beings. Birds and animals, both wild and domesticated, add to the beauty of a household and a village. Man that is said to have been made in God's image is beautiful; and women appear as a comely complement to the beauty that extends much beyond the physical charm. Balmiki's spontaneity in uttering a curse to the hunter was because he was deeply pained seeing one of the pair of birds brought down by the hunter. A hunter killing a bird is natural but Balmiki would not acquiesce in it because disrupting two birds engaged in Beauty's most elevating act - that is love - was not only gruesome but ghastly, too. And when someone kills a love-making soul he cannot escape condign punishment. What is noteworthy is that the punishment is pronounced in the form of poetry.

Kalidas, the poet extraordinaire, had the boon of Goddess Saraswati to become a poet transcending time. Overwhelmed by the presence of Goddess Saraswati, Kalidas sought to sing the Goddess' glory by way of devotion. But what was his first composition? He worshipped Mother Saraswati alright, but he sang of her beauty in a flowing verse. Examples of beauty inspiring timeless poetry multiply. A poet in that way is not his own master; he is at his creative moments overpowered by the twin forces of beauty and love. ``Never durst poet touch a pen to write/Until his ink were temper'd with Love's sighs.'' Poets who are spontaneously pulled to penning love poems can easily realize this Shakespearean verity.

Love seldom communicates; and poets make the inevitable blunder in believing that they are hearing love's murmur that is eminently poetic. In fact, as Shakespeare tells ``...love is blind, and lovers cannot see, the pretty follies that themselves commit.'' But for a poet who receives the blow of love, the ``...feeling is more soft and sensible than are the tender horns of cockled snails.'' The Bard has stated it so succinctly. All poems are a product of love. If there's a poetic call against exploitation it's because the poet loves the downtrodden, if a poem extols people to revolt against terrorism it is the outcome of the poet's love for peace. The same fundamental factor of love applies to poems penned in different times, on different chimes. Perhaps in no other creative channel love predominates so much. What is to be noted is that the poet is not aware that his creative faculty is usurped by some benevolent force and, by the time he comes to understand that his poem has been written while he was in love.

It's a strange experience. Strange - because his creative talents have been utilized without his consent. Falling in love and writing poetry are one and the same thing. Long years ago at a small academic function a woman and I felt the impulse of camaraderie simultaneously. A week later, back at my workplace I received a mobile call from the unknown woman enquiring tidbits about everything but love. I knew her tremulous voice was transmitting sparks of love; I knew I was entering a new phase in my creative career. I wrote my first love poem while she dominated my mind. The next and the fifty odd poems followed as dictated by her delicately. I don't know if she knows what she did, I don't know if I wrote what she wanted me to. Some friends read them and suggested that they were an excellent work of overflowing love. They thought the poems must be shared particularly with those who long for a feel of love.

So, the poems are here; how much love they contain is for the reader to guess.

■

CONTENTS

The First Dawn	21
Smurti – Lingering Past	23
Will You Talk?	25
An Art	27
Crying Clouds	28
Lonely Evening	30
Uncertain Journey	32
Tell-all Silence	33
Can We Dance Again	34
In Flower Garden	37
Graceless Showers	39
Anxiety	41
Meant for You	42
The Konark Tale	44
Spare a Minute	46
Beneath a Tree	48
Jina	50
No Escape	51
Multiple Vision	53
Come for a While	55
Anger	56
Sweetened Emotion	58
(A+B): Math of Life	60
Have I Erred?	61
Please, be Kind	62
Uneasy Lull	63
Between the Lines	64
Glorious Tears	65
Eternal Mirth	67
Paradise	68
Heart's Rhythm	70
False Hope	71

Living in Love	73
Restless Dream	75
Beauty's Everywhere	76
Dream	77
Story of Love	78
Deity of Wilderness	81
Shock of Beauty	83
Uncertain Tide	85
At the Shore	87
Nothing New	88
Yakshya's Curse	89
Delicate Darkness	90
Self-deception	91
Winning Zero	92
Dream and Hope	93
When did You Speak	95
Why Your Lips are shut	97
Faith	98
Dusk and dawn	100
Behind the Glade	101
Tears of June	103
Do You Listen	105
Jina and June	107
Deathless dream	109
Beatific Failure	111
Aradhana	112
Dream and Reality	115
Man's New World	116
Ode to Eventide	118
Glossary	119

EPIGRAPH

Doubt thou the stars are fire;
Doubt that the sun doth move;
Doubt truth to be a liar;
But never doubt I love.

-Hamlet, Act II, Sc. 2, L. 115

The First Dawn

It was the first dawn of creation,
Piercing the thin layers of smog,
Sun's cool beam poured in rays of hope,
The quiet gesture of the overflowing morn
Delivered the message of life,
Humming tunes of hope and delight,

It's a wonderful lonely moment, and
It gets rhythmic in slow scattering beats...
But nothing is cleanly felt, I become
Speechless, and bowing to the sweet serenity
I wait to hear the song of silence,
So fulfilling it is as if set on the Veena,
Here, I wait to see Morning's magnanimity
Along with the flow of a delicate dream,

That afternoon was almost like this
Stuffed with unending pleasant possibilities...
Evading all eyes when you rubbed my palm
Suffusing me with a calm convulsing current...
Pushing me into the
Mesmerizing zone of Cupid's realm,

Since then it has been ringing in my ears...
Building numberless

Castles in my heart… and I stay waiting
To see again that serene solitude…
And amidst all noise
To hear that unsung serenade
From your lustrous lips,

The quiet torture of that un-tuned song
Didn't I know it to linger so long,
Where's its source can't I guess
Does it help to know where it ends?

In my forlorn world, under
Dusk's delicate shade
I feel you subtly leaning…on me
resting your head on my chest.
I guess eon after eon
you are my sweet trail of art
Are you listening my dear,
I offer you Aradhana of my heart…

Smurti — Lingering Past

There she stands alone
Leaning to a slim pillar
Right outside the gate,
Is she waiting for a friend
Or transport,
Because she's late?

I see her there
A cute lovely creature
My eyes refuse to move
What's happening…
I ponder within
Is it the magic of love?

There she stands
Books in hand
The evening is getting dense

And she is alone in the
Waiting shed, don't know
Why I'm getting tense,

Do I know her? No,
Though she studies
In my class,
Now, she seems so dear
And so much near
As if in my heart she's clasped

Let me ask her
If she needs help
Now it is getting late,
Here comes a bus
She gets into it
With a sprightly gait,

Ages have passed…
When I pass that way
I see there she stands
Books in hand blocking
Her bulging bosoms,
A bag from her shoulder hangs,

A feeling so strange
Yet so soothing I can't
Guess any reason
I go that way
I stop there awhile
Season after season…

Will You Talk...

In silence I feel you in my heart
Where else can you reign...
I wonder,
In silence my words are frozen
Yet I try to speak, but lose
My composure,

You don't answer my mails;
Is the address wrong?
You've rendered me less
Serene like an antiquated song,
Amidst all din and clatter
I rush to you, my Dear,
And in uneasy silence
I long for you ever more...

In silence I see both hope
And despair grow,
From my heart you
Emit hope, though
But that evanesces before
Reaching my mind
A stranger I appear to me;
But not to you, I know.

Time passes unbothered,
In doubts I sulk,
In silent adoration I ask:
Can I cajole you to talk…

An Art

She appears,
The quiet portrait of
A flower and tender green foliage:
I am lost in a dilemma.
Will someone tell me
If beauty is beyond smell and touch
Or can be tangible?

There she stands quiet at ease,
But I am motionless, a feeling
Suggests I am in a different world
Overflowing with delight and dilemma
I wonder if beauty can be
Translated into flesh and blood?

Or, if beauty is concealed in my eyes
As philosophers say, how is that
I refuse to turn my face away from
The glare – the gracefully radiant
Cute creature that asks me to
Revise my idea of beauty.

Now I close my eyes, but there she lingers
Not in my eyes but in my heart…
I ponder awhile and whisper to me,
``Look, beauty is an imperceptible art.''

Crying clouds

Rains remind that
The sky too longs for love
By shedding tears of
Passion from above,
Tense clouds fly fast
Pouring torrents of rain
Sailing here and there
Like lovelorn men,

For lovers in rut rains
Bring memories back
In memories lane they
Wander but lose their track,
Such memories are
Stuffed with delicate things
Quietly they delight
The loveless beings,

You can't feel this Jina,
You seem deluded
You think these adulations
Are honestly made!
Who can see love in you,
Who has an inner eye?
Who can bare his heart
And love you as I,

Love has its message
Not always clear
Look at the crying clouds,
Pause a while, Dear,
Lonely evening may mature
Into a restless night
In annoying isolation Jina,
I get a sudden fright.

Lonely Evening

After last night's pleasing showers,
The dawn seems subdued
Like your restrained smile
When you first met me,

I remember that afternoon and the glade
Behind the main college building
We sat on the green carpet,
I reclining to a tree, and
You a metre away, stealthily leering at me,

Do you know how ruddy you had turned,
How overpowered by cheerful shyness!
And how you smiled bashfully reflecting
Your inward joy? I could not read your
Joy that evening beguiled as
I was by the shrinking space between
Your raised knees and your protruding bosoms,

Believe me Jina, your charm had multiplied
many-fold
Though you kept your face buried
In your milk-reddish palms…
Was that reluctance, or was that the
Laconic language of love?

This morning as I see the moistened
Dawn reluctantly brushed over by
The smile of the softening sun
I remember you, my dear, as you melted
Burying your face on my chest...
That evening's hewed in my breast
As this calm morning long years after
That lonely encounter...

For a while I am transported to a new realm
Where I see you as the Jyoti of my mind
And the Laxmi of my heart...
As Jyoti-Laxmi you fly
Like Love's unfailing dart

Uncertain Journey

It seems tiring now after a long walk to moon
Doubts creep in about the promised boon
The goal looks so near, but have I lost my way?
I walk faster but lose the track although you're close by,

Is love a journey so tiring or is it a distant goal?
Sure I walk, and sure I hope but shall I reach at all?
I am a weary soul reduced to skin and bone
I keep breathing and blink and talk to me alone,

Jina, you are winner of hearts
I am under your spell
I wish to breathe and smile and talk
Before going to hell,
Time was I smelled
the Parijata stuck in your bun
Paradise it was I reveled
With you at every turn,

Tired and haggard and worn out
I am helplessly driven
Ask me not, how's the journey
Between hell and heaven.

Tell-all Silence

A soul so sober
A smile so subdued but
So elaborate; only a smile
Can be so emotive, so effusive
I saw you smiling on many occasions
I got to know the enigma called
Love so cutely spoken.

You haven't spoken to me in
Last one year. It's a big gap
Big enough to break the bridge
That joins two passionate hearts.

I could have been a wreck by now
But I am richly nourished by the
Smile that transcends space and silence…
Perhaps I misread your smile Jina
But your silence keeps me going,
Quietly whispering every second
Beat of your heart.

Love is said first
In silence, then in smile,
I was lost in your smile and in your love
There I erred Jina; but now I hear my heart
That feels your tell-all silence
And keep beating in love…

Can We Dance Again

Since morning I am locked indoors
Can't go for a walk
It's sheer boredom Dear
No one here to talk,

Long spell of chilling shower
Makes it a cold gusty day,
With tea and coffee now and then
I am made to stay,

Time was I rejoiced clouds, in rains
I loved to dance
Rains rejoiced seeing us drenched,
Rains too had a chance,

I thought we could dance again
Going back to that year
Those dark clouds those lusty
Rains, can you recall Dear?

Today is Raja festival
I see you on the swing,
How sweetly you fill my heart
Like the festive queen,

That lonely evening in the grove
I was sweetly shocked,
When all of a sudden in your arms
I was cutely locked.

Rains by then had thickened
To give us safety cover,
We forgot to formally thank
The clouds for their timely favour.

Though late let's thank them now
By dancing in rains together,
That may be like telling the rains
We revere their gracious gesture

I think a lot to repay the favour
But no other means I find,
To melt in your arms, Jina,
Has been habit of my mind…

In Flower Garden

More than a flower
You fill the garden,
You choose to move
Among birds alone,
Flowers may rejoice
Getting your company,
Birds may sing sweet
Tunes of harmony,

Twigs come bending flowers
Gaze at your face,
That's the magic of
Your beauty and grace,
You look so singular
Crowned by charm,
As my eyes follow you
I hear my heart's alarm.

I am a feeble soul
I need a bit solace,
Tired, haggard I am
Yet I try to race.
I keep chasing the winner
Whom admirers troll,
Will Jina the winner
Listen to my call?

You look so shiny like
An ever fresh rose,
Your face flashes and
Eyes sparkle in repose,
Are you so engrossed
In you? like the Queen Bee
Here I am near you,
Yet you cannot see.

Unaware, I love you
In garden and in flowers
Doesn't matter whether
You are near me or far.

Graceless Showers

Why rains have become so
Merciless I think I know,
It is not difficult to
Reason out though,
They are graceful
When you are with me,
When you are away
They turn hostile in no time.

Last night showers started
Falling making me restless,
I groped around again and again
Without your trace,
My dream was broken
And my sleep was rudely cleft
Adding to my woes endlessly
The night stretched.

Whole night I thought
You had cursed the rain,
This morning I awaited you
To ring but in vain,
I can't perhaps tell you
How uneasy was the night!
Does it make any sense
To share my grief?

That you don't feel for me
I am not aware,
You seem to be as callous
As the merciless shower,
Rains have stopped meanwhile
But my heart is beating fast
Like the furnace in an
Iron factory that endures a blast.

How long can I absorb the shock I can't say
Seeing no option, Dear I begin to pray.

Anxiety

Earlier I enjoyed your silence
I knew you would talk,
And when you talked so sweetly
I cherished those moments a lot.

I was given to believe
You would buzz and hum,
That would bring love and delight
Mixed with boundless fun.

Now you seldom talk to me
Your silence stabs my passion
Between acute doubt and deep disquiet
I am terribly torn.

Your silence breeds anxiety
With the pressure I can't cope
Anxiety overpowers me, Jina
but I breathe in feeble hope…

Meant for You

Like a chunk of crazy cloud I float around
Preserving all the rains I could,
I float in the sky, I sail here and there
With one aim – to pour all my rains
Wherever I see you...

It doesn't matter what month
What season it is, I care not for
The place - a park, garden or your rooftop
I just look around to see you my dear,
My Jina – all my rains that contain all my love
Is meant for you...

I don't know how long I have to
Run around, I don't know if I chance to
See you now or years later; but one thing:
I won't get tired. My search for you is eternal,
Tireless, and full of hope; I shall find you,
In a desert, in an oasis or elsewhere, but
Wherever you may be you can't be away
From my heart.

I have suffered a lot; but I refuse to stop.
I am sustained not by the sky,
Nor the openness of nature, nor the vast expanse
Nor anything I can think of.

It is you, my Jina
I am living for you only to die for you
After pouring out all my rains – all my
Love - at your feet in the garden
Where you relax in the evening.
True, I am in a state of hopeless
Agitation, but Jina, I am agitated
With a hope to reach you…

The Konark Tale

Returning from Konark disappointed
At Ramachandi Poet Neelakantha rested
Students from Satyabadi accompanied him
They had gone to see Konark in moon-lit evening
But heavy pouring frustrated their tour
They ran back to find a safe shelter.

Can we see Konark when
The moon's in full bloom?
The poet and his pupils
Sighed in gathering gloom.

Konark is a sad tale of celestial whim
When the Sun god's temerity brought his ruin
He chased Chandrabhaga the Saint's daughter
The bride rejected the Sun as her suitor
The Saint came to know of the Sun's impudence
He cursed the Sun and the temple crashed hence.

That's a sad tale that cautions
Lovers to be prudent,
Not to proceed in love
Without the bride's consent.

The tale comes to mind as I see the rains
And my castle that remains intact in heavens
It's with Jina's consent I built the castle
No threat to its safety, it will never fall.

Now rains have stopped
There is hope in the horizon,
But without Jina by my side
I see my hopes are frozen.

Spare a Minute

You have robbed smile off my face
Filled my heart with sorrow,
Alone I walk a crowded path
But nowhere can I go,
None can hear my heart's wail
I can't tell anyone
A lonely soul I keep walking
Talking to me alone…

Will you spare a minute,
Will you await a while?
I know it means nothing to you
All I say is futile,
But you can look back Jina
To see you in my arms
You may pretend that I am wrong
But you can't forget the charm.

That's now thing of the past
But past tends to repeat
At times it repeats as a tragedy
At times it's a treat.

That day begun with roses smiling
I heard flowers rhyme,

You filled my heart with your music
My day passed like a poem.

Can you hear me now, Jina
Do you think of us
Those moments of love, and personal bliss
Or you see them only as dross?

I have lost a lot Jina, sure
You have gained nothing,
Are you enjoying my discomfiture
Staring from the fringe?

Beneath a Tree

Tree is the most beautiful poetry, it is said
True, the beauty unfolds when read
I see you standing at a tree like a lyrical tune
Quietly overflowing with music in raga unknown.

You remind of Kilmer and Omar Khayyam
Those immortal souls sang tree's paean
They saw tree as symbol of life and love,
And as Nature's greatest gift all above…

About tree Joyce Kilmer wrote immortal lines
He thought a tree was a thing Divine
To him the tree was an art of God
A tree may be essayed in letters of gold.

Omar Khayyam saw tree as an ideal place
Where he and his sweetie could revel and rest
I love to read those lines to you
They always inspire as eternally new:
"Here with a loaf of bread beneath the bough
A flask of wine, a book of verse and thou,
Beside me singing in the wilderness
And wilderness is Paradise anew."

Beneath the tree I see you by my side,
For a while keeping all mundane things aside,
Gracefully you rest your left arm on its branch
I lock you in my eyes and fall into a pleasant trance.

Clad in oblong stripes of black and red
You appear to have been divinely made
Your beauty adds soul to solitude
The prelude I try to sing but not the postlude.

Jina*

It's two years since we met last
Sweetly I am caught in time past
Time present brings hope for future
Some day you will smile, I am sure,

How trying it is to live in hope and tear
To drag weary legs to that warm winter
Where you met me first in the noisy corridor
Where you promised a lot, but did you deliver?

Caught in endless gloom I take a factual view
But mind refuses to listen, the heart cries for you,

Cuddling you in heart is itself a reward
It feels the momentum of moving forward
But don't I know where indeed I am led
Sure, I am not stagnant, but am I inching ahead?

How blissful it is to hear the music of love
Even while roasted in a smoldering stove
You are muse and music set in Veena
Winner of hearts you are, I name you Jina…

Jina means winner of hearts

No Escape

You have been the cloud
Over my head,
Shielding me from the
Sun wherever I tread,
I feel you but never
Look above,
I do not want to be
Face to face with love.

You are the rosy sprig I see in the park
You are the full-blown rose I see in dark
You are the rose with elegant thorn
More confused I am the more I learn.

Like a lotus bud unfolding in the pond
Your smile I enjoy but nothing beyond
You are so far yet so near you seem
In my hopeless heart like soothing moon beam…

Often I try to read words of your eyes
I can't decipher them I am not that wise
Howsoever I think you remain a puzzle
A lovelorn soul I am you make me vulnerable.

I see you there happy teaching your class
Helplessly, Dear I stay untaught, alas!
Will you teach me the lesson I want to learn
Can I learn if you leave me alone?

You are Jina the winner
Here I am left to rot,
Where can I escape?
In a hopeless maze I am caught.

Multiple Vision

Harsh summer has come
No respite from heat
Last winter's warmth, however,
Remains a lovely treat
Winter became warm
When you touched my heart
It remains as warm as ever as
Love's impassioned art?

Months have passed,
The affinity seems to rise,
It's my sole possession
And greatest prize
You promised a lot –
Heaven to earth everything,
But all these days
You delivered nothing.

I see you floating in
Mind's multiple vision,
But quietly you evanesce
Like a cute illusion,
Sure I think
You are real to me,
But from my heart and soul
Suddenly you flee.

My heart feels the tears I shed for you
Where can you hide you have options few
Elsewhere I may err but here there's no error
In silence I suffer longing for you ever more.

Love is an elusive promise amidst anxiety
Like the fear to get exposed amidst false vanity.

I look back to see I was a neat gainer,
So cool you are now and so warm in winter.

Come for a While

It's a pleasure to keep waiting for you
At times it seems disheartening though
Between hope and despair I am torn
Can you imagine how poignantly I am forlorn?

Your pride of beauty makes you haughty
It pains me to think but you're ungracefully naughty
How this happens, Jina I fail to reason
It's not the right course that you have chosen.

Endlessly I may have to wait for you
Now hope… now despair that's my due
Hope and despair do not matter to me,
I wait no matter how tasking time may be.

Years ago I rejoiced the pledge of your love
Years ago I guess you were the symbolic dove
So cute and so caring you were then
Sure I am, you will respond again.

Intervening silence could be sweet in love
But in too much silence affinity may dissolve
I have suffered silently in flickering hope
It's pleasantly hypnotic as if I am doped.

You are so moony in your smile,
End this wait dear come for a while.

Anger

Before seeing you I was wary of anger
It is defined in texts as mischief monger,
Losing one's cool is an unmanly act
Anger is man's enemy as a matter of fact.

You have been a smiling deity to me
I thought, come what may angry you won't be,
Then I tried to imagine how you will look
When I make you angry by hook or by crook…

Such things I often think about you
When you come you steal away all I knew,
That day you seemed upset and tense
I was concerned who gave you offence.

But soon I was transfixed seeing your face
Anger had multiplied your innate grace,
Your cheeks had reddened like morning sun's rays
Your eyes were fuming with lovely ruddy rage.

Your rosy lips throbbed but you said nothing
Your brows were knitted with light sweating,
I can't find words to say how you looked
While looking for words again I got hooked.

I stood motionless like an autumn reed
I tried to steal your anger but did not succeed,
I wonder and wonder how anger adds to your grace
Howsoever I try, the reason I fail to trace.

Sweetened Emotion

I have roamed a lot
In terrains, mountains, meadows,
In dales and vales,
In caves and crags,
With a lonely heart,
Peeping into hopeless future,
I keep roaming here and there
Although I know where you are…

It can't be that you have forgotten
That winter…the evening
That brought us together…
I am lost in the past,
What have I to look forward to?
The future appears bleak,
The present unbearable
It's the past that keeps me throbbing,
Because you were there…

If you are not with me everything appears pale,
I hold you in my heart, that's all I can do,
The feeling is so soothing. But my anxiety grows
And I talk to me,
Can you hear when I call you from my heart?
Why then in silence so cruelly do you act?

You have won me Jina,
You know that...by losing to you
I win my most prized possession...

I understand your queries
But you do not my worries
Like a split cloud I run
My grief nowhere to unburden
Where will I rest at last?
Rest for me was pleasure of the past...

True, the sweetened emotion comes as a blow
I desist from telling you what you neatly know...

(A+B): Maths of Life

Someone said you teach science
Chemistry, botany but not mathematics
For you (A+B) functions may mean nothing
For me they amount to one and the only thing...

`A' for me is Aradhana...Love and Adoration
`B' is Bina that puts the feeling to tone
Aradhana and Bina both you are to me
Science or what else your subject may be.

For me you are the subject Supreme
You are Love's lyrics you're crème de la crème
You fill me with something I can't narrate
You are my finest pleasure and rarest rest.

A weary soul I am beholden to you
You are there in whatever I view
Where I am being led I can't really guess
Left to your care I feel happy and fresh.

(A+B) contains Life's full equation
I gaze at you and see a happy transition,
You are my elixir may I pronounce thrice:
You are the symbol of all that's nice...

Have I Erred?

The sky looks empty and meaningless
I saw clouds sailing and the moon
Peeping through the east,
I feel restless like that puranic bird
That finds a meaning in water when it rains.

Clouds sail lustily, there's calm around
Like your lovely form, your innate charm,
Your heart-winning presence,
Your beguiling demeanour
But lost I am in graceful rains
Because you are not here…

The calm afternoon makes me sad
You are away dear, rains make me mad
This and that about you I keep on mulling
I don't notice the clouds but rains keep falling.

I ponder now and again but have no answer
What can be my lapse, where have I erred?

Please, be Kind

Carefree you put on a red saree
You appear beauty perfect
Other women are readers' poetry
You are poetry of poets…

Poetry, they say, is spontaneous flow
Mixed with love it becomes a sweet blow,
I preserve your blows with a lot of care
Your punches are hard but they don't scare.

I miss you Jina for no reason it seems
Love has no reason that's what it means,
You think you will run leaving me behind
I keep pleading, my Dear, please be kind.

Love is not a carefree song it has a fixed metre
It's song of sweet dream, it's not a nightmare.

Uneasy Lull

As I rise you rush in like delight of the dawn
Happily confused I hear the quiet tune of morn
I know you are my only music, my only adoration
Morning, evening, night and day you are my sole mission.

Day breaks with love to you day passes with love
Evening sings cool serenade night comes with hope,
Night deepens and hope grows pale and starts pinching
It's so bitter and so painful like a brutal lynching.

How long may I singe in love I see no way out
It's beyond what heart can bear but I can't even shout,
In silence I see you, dying for the dark night to pass
Will the morning come I get flurried, alas!

I am a luckless zero without you, my heartbeat you are
To you can I open my heart with none else can I share,
My misfortune's my own my tears I can't wipe
In sad isolation I suffer in ceaseless painful strife.

How warm are my tears that flow invisible to all
Can't you see my sullen heart and its uneasy lull?

Between the Lines

I thought you were temperate spring
Stuffed with vernal pleasure,
You are answer to nature's caprice
In simple amiable measure.

I see your eyes fixed on me like
Sun flower gazing at the sky,
Your smile seems so inviting
Signaling hi…hi…hi
You avoid direct eye contact
But the corner of your look,
Says so much in so many words
It's like a warm absorbing book.
In silence I am absorbed in you,
If you know it's fine,
Someday when your heart beats for me
Read me between the lines…

I clasp you closely a burning flame
Your limbs defy nature's rule,
A torch of fire you're
Can't guess how you're so cool.

Glorious Tears

At times I feel my eyes getting wet
I wish to dismiss tears before I am upset
In vain I try those memories to efface,
The more I try the more they surface…

Tears have their ways to tell the tale
Now they create heaven…now the hell,
That winter evening was Heaven's delight
The touch of passion remains my finest gift.

Passion sagged soon after… hell followed in
Like a spring evening lashed by turbulent rain,
I am left to muse what mistake I made
Did I miss the warning in the script I read?

Punishment without offence's terrible to take
What have I done I wonder, what's my mistake
No one to tell… tears have no voice
Left to sulk and suffer… I have no choice.

Spring came, then summer I was left to rot
Seasons show their wrath often unsought,
I am left to suffer, it seems quite an ordeal
Yet I enjoy the pain with a pleasure drill.

Should I let tears refresh love's cruelty?
Is it love or my folly, what's the reality?
Must I stay caught in massive isolation?
The cut is most unkind without any reason
Tears unseen flow inside my heart
Helplessly I am bound in a passionate trap.

Yet, passionate past is quietly a treasure trove
Glorious are the tears of adoration in love…

Eternal Mirth

The path to wisdom lies through love
After lot of thinking Sant Kabir said so,
I thought you will teach me the truth
Of life and love and eternal mirth…

Instead you taught me to build a castle
In the air without any hassle,
How quickly such castles are built
Amazing how animated was I to the hilt.
The castles I made still hangs in air
Can I live in it if you are nowhere?

The castles appears like an organic body
For life to spring, it has everything ready,
But can a body breathe to life sans a heart
The castle I try to enter but my life falls apart.

It's a fabulous castle but what's its worth?
Getting into it without you I am loath,
Mechanically, Jina I continue to breathe
In the huge green expanse like a useless heath.

Paradise

Can you say how it started…
How it grew so fast,
It seems ages to me though
Just two years have passed.
I store that evening in by breast
That winter breeze,
I feel your palm touching mine
In serene surprise,

The soft touch was warm enough
To give love's tingling message,
A week or more I stayed enthralled
Nibbling love's sausage.
Around that time one morning
Came your first mobile call,
I danced in ecstasy and joyfully
Forgetting all my trouble…

There's magic in your face,
Magnet in your words
There's something I can't name,
That's my best reward.
Near or far doesn't matter
You're music to my ear,
Limpid lyrics you are to me
Wherever you are.

The more I lose myself the more I read of you,
Reading letters of love alone is pleasure anew,
For weeks, months a full year I built my paradise
Where we roamed and reveled carefree and ease.

Time past now invades me I feel deeply sad,
I try to escape but can't move forward or backward...

Heart's Rhythm

At times you make me restless
I rush to see you in blood and flesh
You fill both my awareness and dream
How you do so I can't imagine.

You don't know what you are to me
The air of my breath, my heart's rhythm,
In you my mind often loses its way
I don't try to restrain and enjoy going stray,

How nice it is to float in happy unknown
In that forgetful lake I love to drown,
Drown or float doesn't matter much
If you do not leave me in the lurch,

Living or dying is no more a big deal
My awareness and dream both you steal,
When you steal I gain a lot by losing
You are the stealer that itself is amusing,
You are around that offers a promise
Can you leave me Jina, I can't believe.

You are the mainstay in awareness and dream
I see you dear in both milk and cream.

False Hope

The other day I roamed
On the Hooghly shore,
Coolly I started thinking
About you more and more,
There's nothing else
That fills my mind
For you, dear I have left
Everything behind…

I cry and cry hiding, unseen
To me and others,
I feel the bleeding of my heart
No one sees my tears,
How you can't get to know
How I am dying for you,
Won't you stop a while and
Ring before bidding adieu?

Can you live leaving me away
Won't you miss me Dear,
I can't thrive even for a minute
If you are not here,
How I breathe, and eat and sleep

I am not aware,
In vain do I reason saying
In love everything's fair.

You are away Jina dear false hope sustains me,
I'll await you dear how harrowing it may be.

Living in Love

I wonder how benignly you smile
You are my joy forever,
To my life you have lent fragrance
With Love's eternal flavor,
When I murmur, `I love you Jina'
I see you smile and smile
I lose my heartbeats and merge in you
And stay merged for a while.

Unaware, I learn from you the charm
Of living in love,
Teach me more of what you know
Knowing me to be a docile dove...

I adore you as the Goddess of Love
I deify you in my soul,
In this world and beyond dear
You are my only goal,
I may go to the other world
Following Nature's law,
Can you linger here without me
That, I am sure, you know.

Come and join me Jine
A minute seems a year now,
I'll bare my heart and tell
All I hold for you.

I wait for you Jina you are my only joy
To breathe in love I've no option, no other way.

Restless Dream

It little comforts me to chase
You closing my eyes,
In your office chamber, in your
Class room where you teach
Science…or in the play ground
Where you oversee the school
Annual sports.

Perhaps you don't know how restless
I am and how anxious I get when
I fail to see you…you are but a
Dream for me and in my dreamland
You fill everything - the lake, the valley,
The grove, the hillock – and the void
That dissolves when my dream breaks.

When love beckons - each breath
Becomes dreamy, and every object
Becomes an image… Aware or unaware
I am drawn to the land of dreams and
Sleep eludes me throwing open a vast expanse,
Where the Fairy Queen moves with her
Elegant gait. It's a fabulous sight; and
Slowly I am drawn into a novel domain
When you close me in your warming bosom.

Beauty's Everywhere

You taught me to see beauty in you,
Now I see nothing anywhere
Am I in a magic world,
And none but Adoration abides there…

I've travelled a lot in streets,
And towns, in rivers and in air
In dreams and delicate pastures, alone
Wherever I am invisibly you are there.

In vain do I rush to the corridor,
Where you roamed in artistic flair
I am lost in your smile and eyeful gesture
Is it because you are not there?

Adore beauty and adore you it's all the same
You remain so sweet, so beautifully serene.

Dream

Clad in exquisite black saree over your shoulder
It adds to your luster with green golden border,
Your glistening face contrasting black bristling hair
Dainty dark sky and mirthful moon both you are…

The gold chain is lucky that bedecks your neck
So is black elegant blouse that covers your chest,
You are music to me and you are lyrics
I see you in my heart no need to open my eyes…

Your profile dazzles with your surreal smile
Your eyes tell what your closed lips try to conceal,
Oh, I wonder how Beauty could so fluently talk
I can follow the train it's my sheer good luck…

A slim basket pressed to your slender waist
How nimbly your fingers clutch its edge,
The delicate knuckles and the fist so sober
The sure passionate grip to restrain a lover…

True, I miss you… but I am not sad
As I write, your dream supplies every word.

Story of love?

You are a winner Jina your prowess
None can challenge,
None can make you snigger and smile
Unless you yourself crave.

I see you there so sober a figure
So gracious, so pleasing
You are amiable and benign too
But aren't you amazing?

I see you angelic in blissful dream
I ask you to tarry a while,
As the moon fades and night retreats
You recede a thousand miles.

It seems an illusion Jina
In my heart I feel you well,
I can't touch you or talk to you
All my efforts I fail.

You appear and leave yet you linger
Do you play hide and seek?
You arrive now and vanish next
As if in a flick.

I long for you, you keep me waiting
Is it the story of love?
For an answer I am dying Dear
Nothing in me evolves.

Deity of wilderness

Alone on the river bank
You are photographed,

Like a Deity of wilderness,
In a crowd among friends
You look so shining and alluring,
Here alone... all alone you look
So placid, but irresistibly seductive...

You are made to be impressed in heart
Or locked in an admiring eye; how unfeeling
If the finger that clicked the camera to
Capture you in its reel. The photographer
Seems to be happy, so the camera's dark box,
But here I fail to reason how the jewel of
My heart will be imprisoned in a heartless camera
That understands nothing of a lover's heart.

I may look for answer, but where's a passionate heart
That can clear my doubt?
I am wallowing in confusion Jina: how can you,
The Deity of wilderness be a photo subject
That too while emitting beauty all around.

Sure, you have agreed, I know, you are
Generous to make your admirers happy,
But my heart is bleeding, I am not your
Admirer Jina because a loving heart
Doesn't admire but adore…

Seeing your ruddy ravishing splendor
The river has forgotten to flow,
The evening is at hand dear
But the sun has started to glow…

The sun's act is admirable but that's
No answer to my confusion,
Why didn't the Sun god intervene…
To stop the camera with a stern caution?

Shock of Beauty

When an eager heart seeks solitude
Beauty manifests herself in many ways,
Where solitude breeds fear in heart
Beauty turns shocking and rude,

The shock of beauty I had years ago
It was so quick and sudden and deep,
But there was something new and novel
That tremor and thrill I can't forgo.

From the sparse crowd she emerged
She smiled and signaled, I took the call
I felt a kind of bonhomie and intimacy
With her will, I readily merged…

Now I feel the parting pang the merger seems to crack
Where to go and where you are I am in dark.

Uncertain Tide

A lovely river you are flowing into my dream,
But never do you sweep me in your lovely stream.

I love to get drowned in your bosom,
But you keep me teasingly waiting,
I am pushed into a delicate dilemma
Do you want me to stay floating?

Just floating with hope to join you some day
Crossing impassable obstacles on the way.
How long will it take I can't guess
May be while I am alive or after my death,
Beauty's eternal blaze I adore in your glare
Even if I am dazzled by I intently stare

Your admirers may have made you proud
In beauty's fiery flood many might have drowned
Shall I reach the shore or receive a nasty blow?
I care not for the end in the stream I flow…

I watch the river but know not when the tide is turning
Now or later but sure I keep my hope burning.

At the Shore – You Are

I saw the clouds sailing across
And the moon gliding with them,
I thought you are running to me
But I was mistaken.

Waiting for your arrival is
More anxiety than an option
Should I hasten to you instead
But how fast can I run?

Anxiously awaiting you for years
I am getting tired,
Time passes fast, hope withers
I find me nowhere.

Are you relaxed without me,
Can't you hear my call?
A shipwrecked marooned in the sea
Nothing have I at all.

I forget the danger and impending
Death, I hold on to life
At the shore you are waiting for me
Do I care for this strife!

Nothing New

I take it as a boon that my
Heart is bleeding for you
You know but pretend not to see
For you it's nothing new,
Love frozen in my heart
Has made me languidly lazy
But I do everything outward
To keep myself busy...

I dream eyes-closed though inwardly wide awake
I don't open my eyes because love's reward's at stake
I fear you may vanish if I open my eyes
Reality means little and dream quietly dries.

You will come! I can't dare to dream
A great dreamy reward it is - you are mine,
I am helpless I have no say on dream
It comes and flows me on a sober stream.

Floating in dream I know from the very start,
Dreams don't drown a loving heart...

Yakshya's Curse

The Yakshya was imprecated to live alone
Bereft of his consort in a hilly zone
After summer, clouds sailed scattering rains
The Yakshya beheld the clouds and cried again.

`Take a message to my lovely bride'
Pleading to clouds the Yakshya cried
`Your message will be carried we are ready,'
Clouds asked how to spot the winsome lady.

Yakshya gave an account of his beloved consort
`She shines like jewel,' said the Yakshya:
`Deep's her naval cavity
Marvelous her slender waist
And she is bent a little on her midriff
With pleasing pressure of her chest...'

Kalidas's Meghadoot comes to mind
Seeing the clouds floating behind
Huge boulders on the river bank seem to say
They are happy and they enjoy your stay

You are tale of waves
You have lot more tales in store,
Waves have stopped to hear
Your tales and see you ever more...

Delicate Darkness

I love dreaming you in the dark
Closing my eyes to all other things
Darkness fills my heart with hope
Telling me you are mine…

I don't know how dreams creep in
Or how you enter my heart,
You are subtle sweetness, dear
You have mastered the art.

I love dreaming you in day light
Keeping my eyes open,
Slowly the day turns awesome
Always does it happen…

Day or night or dawn or dusk
I feel you plundering my heart,
How painfully you keep me dreaming
How pleasantly you depart!

Did I say you enter my heart?
Yet I hugely I err,
Why should you enter a niche
Where you are always there.

Self-deception

My pretension doesn't let me cry
I can't deceive myself howsoever I try
I restrain my wet eyes from shedding tears
Your agonizing silence is painful to bear
I pose as a mature man with a smile alright
But let me confess I suffer from a fright.

No doctor can diagnose my sad confession
Quietly I conduct myself in fake fashion
But I can't deceive you with my concocted smile
You know why I cry and why you stab me to wail.
I wait to hear from you where did I err?
You say nothing and never do you stir.

I open the file but can't send you message
Can I ring you? No…not at this stage!
Your options are open, my hands are tied
A friend enquired this morning to him I lied.

I shed tears hoping you will get to feel
My eyes do not cry, but my heart does wail.

Winning Zero

It feels so nice to lose
A point to your cute ruse
How thrilling it is to say
You have beaten me to joy.

This is the magic of emotion
That knows nothing but passion
That feels happier after a loss
Seeing you beaming with winning gloss.

But know it dear your triumph
Is not as pleasant as my defeat,
I lose to you but feel a winner
It's pleasing to become a defeated hero.

A positive digit you are also a winner,
I help you multiply tenfold by being a zero…

Dream and Hope

In dreary desert of Corona crisis
You continue to console like an oasis
The pandemic lurks around here and there
With you Jina by my side I don't care.

Corona restrains my speed
Keeping me alone indoors,
But my heart races to you
Accelerating ever more...

Do I reach you, I don't know
Do you hear me ever?
Restless soul I am, I cry
Seeking a bit succour...

My comforting touch you are
You are my only cheer,
How sweetly my heart beats, Jina
Because you are there!

It's a pleasure to think
You will one day hear,
Doesn't matter in dream or reality
You'll come near.

It will be a long wait I know
It may stretch till morn,
The dream shall end and hope rise
And love shall make me learn.

Can you look the other way
When I call you to come,
In love I dream, in love I hope
Is it a magic run?

When Did You Speak?

When did you speak to me last?
Seems yesterday only, though it's years past
My time stands still listening to your voice
I have no option Dear, nowhere can I rejoice.

I preserve your long mobile call
I miss your sweet tone,
I still can hear you cooing
`I love you too' alone.

Never can I believe,
You have forgotten those days,
Those delightful afternoons, and
The evening breezes,
I am sure you long for them
Those days I sorely I miss,
Don't you feel, for us those days
Remain eternal bliss.

You broke away Jina, the shock was so sudden
Sorrow overshadows me I can't relieve my burden.

Why Your Lips are Shut

A listless afternoon, in the corridor of hope
With a happy mind I got a mild shock
You came so near I can't believe now
Now I am bewildered; where're you?

I remember your smile and
The endearing hint,
I preserve the sequence
And your passionate glint,
A lonely soul I am aloof
From friends and colleagues,
Alone I walk a crowded path
No more in the same league.

I see no escape from despair…
No one can I talk,
Lost in a cruel world I am
Held at an unyielding block…
Will time change, in vain
I keep hoping,
Hoping against hope in dark
I keep groping.

In some hope and little anxiety I am made to rut
Your eyes say a lot Jina, why your lips are shut?

Faith

Last morning you mailed
Saying it was all delight,
So lovely was that to make
My day exquisitely bright...
I paused a while to ponder
If you are so busy,
Why no mails from you today
I feel so uneasy.

For you it may not mean
Much to write a word to me,
When you do not write dear
It feels my heart is drying,
Slowly I come to see you
As my life and death
Are you ever aware Jina,
You're my life breath?

Do I breathe happily,
Do I live in cheer?
I wait for you Jina,
My call, can't you hear?

You are the winner of hearts Jina
You are a lover's dream,
You are the river…you are the lake
You are the pious stream.

I wait for you with hope and fear
I wait holding my breath,
I don't fall or crumple or flounder
Because I am sustained by faith…

Dusk and Dawn

At dusk you rush in and retreat at dawn
Can't I guess, what's the game?
You are in my arms Jina though the spatial
Stretch remains the same.

Four hundred miles from Hooghly to Brahmani
From my garden house to your school,
There you teach science of Nature's secret
And subtly make me miserable.

Do you know the secret of Nature,
Life's concealed message?
Nature rests on cycle of seasons,
On love life rests always.

True, I haven't cried Jina
But my heart never stops bleeding,
In hope and despair now and then
I just keep pleading.

If you hear me pining for you
It's my telepathy,
If you pretend you feel nothing
It's your sheer apathy.

Behind the Glade

It rained this afternoon
From my south facing balcony
I saw the South City
Engulfed in a thick blanket of
Serene showers…

Here are bunches of burning Gulmohar
Relishing the rare touch of rain,
Reclining on an easy chair here
I long for a sprinkle in vain.

Oh, a great afternoon it is
It takes me back to my club creek,
Where alone behind the glade
You pressed your lips on my cheek.

Keeping a gap between your lips
you ran your tongue this way that way,
That was a glorious feeling Jina
I preserve that till this day.

A small touch on my cheek
My whole body quivered,
Like a tender banana leaf
In soft autumn air.

Then you expected me to act but
I couldn't return your kiss,
Till today I get thrilled about the evening
And the occasion I missed.

Couldn't put my lips on that rosy cheek
That looked so ruddy in gloaming,
The setting sun seemed staring at us,
And my heart was throbbing.

Tears of June

Robert Burns reminds of love
With the arrival of June
He tells of the red red rose
To a lover that is known
``My love is like a red red rose,''
sang he, ``That's newly sprung in June,
O' my love's like the melodie
That's sweetly played in tune.''

To me June is a fabulous month
Though it's high summer
You're cool breeze amidst heat,
Gift of June you are.

Five decades ago mid-June
You came to earth,
A cute occasion it was
When love took new birth.

A child dazzle you were
You had a winning stare,
You won friends, admirers,
And chasers everywhere.

In school, college and markets
Wherever you trod,
Your friends and colleagues
All loved to walk that road.

Over the years you grew up
Beauty to beauty, by Jove
Years later I saw you
As symbol of beckoning love.

You have kept me waiting
Can you count the years?
Painful wait it is, Dear
Can't you feel my tears…

Do You Listen?

Do you listen to me Jina
What I speak,
Or you just listen to what I say
But the import you skip.

You are an adept in posturing
I can't dispute your show,
You smile and in meaty silence
Quietly you create a row.

I am bewitched by your smile
By your silence I am miffed,
Pushed into a dejection zone
My heart has been ripped.

My broken heart I can't show others
That you pretend not to see,
If you're happy to see me shattered
That's happiness for me.

There's a pleasure in hoping
When everything goes wrong,
Hope keeps me alive here
To the place I don't belong.

Where to go and where to rest
If you are not with me,
No escape from chasing torture
Where can I flee?

There I look and there you are
In confusion I am caught,
I run to you, shall keep running
You are my resting slot…

Jina* and June

March is the month of war
April is cruelest, they say,
May's hot, June sends showers
As prelude to June comes May…

I don't curse May's heat
Absorbed as I am in June
June is the month of Jina
That puts rains to tune.

In my south facing balcony I sit
Hoping for a soft shower bath,
Clouds fail me now and then
Is that Jina's wrath?

Can I ask Jina to explain…
Her sudden change of mood,
So dear and so darling she is
Why has she become so rude?

No mobile call, no message
No contact of any kind,
I'm sure she reminisces all
Yet I seek to remind.

In a benign June she was born
Years have passed since then,
As a sweet tune she stays in me
I can't recall since when.

Now floats grey clouds of June
I hear their drizzling whisper,
Listen to the call of clouds, Jina
To me you're always so dear…
----
*Jina is winner of hearts

Deathless Dream

The sky looks so faded today
The clouds seem to have been tired,
It is raining in rhythm, however
With occasional burst of thunder,
But I am absorbed in the lightning
That reminds of the feminine glamour
That is so natural to you…

Under an overcast sky,
Seeing the rapturous rains
Irresistibly lashing the lush green
Cover of the meadow, I fall into
A reverie: I am drawn into my young days
When you made me taste the nectar
Of love.

In dreams you made me sleep
In another world, and awake in the dawn
I was made to believe that we would
Fly to a far-off world – an Eden
Where love reigns supreme comforting
The passionate souls.

Oh, that was a dream – there was no
Reason for the dream to die,

After decades of loveless existence
I tell myself: Every death is painful;
Every death diminishes God
And in the process love is diminished;
But when dreams die
Death becomes endless...

It's miserable to live and not dream
But in misery I see you there,
I keep going and shall go on
Till you come and draw me into
A dream concealed in your smile,
Your fig-leaf hesitancy, and your
Simulated reluctance...

Beatific Failure

It's beatific failure,
It pinches a lot, so subtle
And so painful. Yet it emits hope;
The pain can't be shared with any,
And the hope no one can share.
It's fragile and so piercing, I can't
Keep it in me, I can't conceal
It from others, my fading feature,
My drooping eyes reveal what
You only know.

Hope may escape any time
Leaving me neither here nor anywhere,
But I have to breathe, I've no choice.
You may perhaps say you are sorry;
That's your escape route.
But do you need to escape, Jina?
No, you need not.
I need to get out of this blind alley
But I cannot.

It's futile you seek reprieve
You are the only woman I love Jina,
You are the only woman I can't forgive.

Aradhana*

A subtle touch…
Quietly I get the feel
How soft your palm could be!

The selfie was taken,
The sun sank slowly
The dusk seemed exotic but cold…
We dismissed the freezing chill
Winter kept us warm
Your soft cuddle had its magic hold,

It's a year now, we haven't met
Yet you persist in me…
In my arms…
In my dreams…and in finest intimacy…

Is it love, I ask. Can you hear me?
Three hundred days have passed…
Maybe it is long enough a gap
But nothing of that evening has lapsed,

I feel the warmth of your body
And Love's serenade I hear,
You are four hundred miles away, Dear
But I relish your lisping whisper,

In dainty dreams I lose myself
In deep warm embrace in your bosom,
Amidst pitch dark night, I pine for you
That may be love, I presume

But I can't be sure
It could be adoration, I guess…
It's Adoration – Aradhana…
In all my being subtly I rejoice,

That I define as love; 'No, it wasn't,'
You seem to caution me…
I am puzzled and I ponder awhile
What else could it be! …

I feel you breathe
Whiffs of tepid air into my breast
And nibble around my nape…
How delicate your rosy lips,
Your blushing chin
You rub in the furrow of my chest…

In whisper you seem to say:
Love is not love if it fails to beat a winter…
With kisses, embraces, and lusty grips
And yet something more…

Love's a thrill of mutual consent, but
Aradhana is one's own,
I wait for your arrival Dear, before
To the Seventh Heaven I am flown

Come, O` bonny bride, give your hand
Let's be one before a selfie is clicked…
The bliss that flows from Adoration
No mundane love could fleece…

That's Aradhana…my Aradhana…and Aradhana for ever
Placid Adoration it is, it keeps flowing winter, spring and summer.

----

*Aradhana is adoration in love.

Dream of Reality

How I long to see you… and see you
And feel you as my breath!
You lend meaning to my feelings
Making love my faith,
I see you as the gift of heaven
You are the evening star,
You seem so captivating and close
Yet so elusive and rare…

I am involved in your `hide and seek'
I do not know if I seek or I hide,
In hiding I enjoy seeking you
The tiny bashful bride,
It's a mesmeric state I know
I am in a state of flux,
Now you're there now you vanish
In vain do I rush.

But you are now right here
I don't know how to act,
You are here in flesh and blood
Yes, that's a fact.

How a dream becomes so real
I cannot imagine,
With you by my side Jina
Reality seems a dream.

Man's New World

Where's a resting place?
Where one can breathe,
And with eyes closed can
think thoughts
without fear?
And thank the heavenly father that
All's well here and everywhere,

Decades ago a poet dreamt of
Such a place,
Bothered by a divided world,
He prayed and sought God's grace,
He prayed for a world not fragmented by
``Narrow domestic walls,''
Where man can breathe free air, and
Speak out his mind without inhibition and fear.

That was a century ago,
Time has moved fast since then,
Man has acquired both knowledge
And technology to live a cozy life
Unimaginable any time in history;
The search for a better life is over
Now it is time to enjoy the fruits of
Knowledge. Machines are employed

To run man's errands, and modern
Gadgets with their artificial mind
Are ever ready to give man whatever
He wants. Oh, great time indeed!

``We have heaven on earth, we have created
The heaven here," said he to the poet.

But have you retained God's great gift,
That's love?

You have created heaven on earth!
Not a mean achievement,
Friend, said the poet,
Just pause a while…
Can you breathe clean air
in this man-made heaven?
Can you taste clean water?
Can you see stars in the firmament?
Can you enjoy good health?
And sing to yourself?

Can you sing a prayer shedding
A tear drop for God?
Can you feel love in your heart
That's life's best reward?

It's man's new world of all earthly comfort,
It's a world man prides on but love's lost...

Ode to Eventide

In the summer evening I sat alone
Relaxed I was the day's work was done
The light south breeze brought restful cheer
To see the sinking sun I stepped out of door
In my garden it was a riot of flowers
I sat stretching my legs in an easy chair.

The Sun rises in the morning in evening he rests
His path from east to west is easily traced
His is a lovable travel full of life and mirth
Every day he travels cheerily on the same path
It's a path of love one travels in same fashion
Never getting bored never curtailing motion,

Love's the fuel that propels me to streak
Without a moment's rest without a break
Don't know how Jina ignites my mind
I walk forward by looking behind.

It's a pleasure to keep walking in love
In deserts, oceans and air around the globe
How long can I walk I don't know
To walk is the debt to love I owe.

Not much hope I see in the loveless world
Yet, ecstasy it is in love to dream forward.

Glossary

Aradhana: A feeling of great love or worship. Also, a desire to get absorbed in a symbol that signifies love. Seen as Aradhana, love becomes a dignified feeling.

Bina: A common feminine name in Odisha and India. Bina (commonly spelt Veena) is a musical instrument that produces a mellifluous tune.

Brahmani: A river in eastern Odisha that is as intimidating when flooded as it is saddening when it dries up in summer months. It reflects the two extreme states of emotion.

Gulmohar: Unlike common flowers that bloom in gardens, Gulmohar unfolds its petals high on twigs of tall trees. Seeing Gulmohar blossoms gives a thrill like falling in love.

Chandrabhaga: Daughter of a sage who lived with her father in a hermitage near the Sun temple, Konark. The sun god wooed her, blown by her ravishing beauty. She spurned his overtures because while the sun god was stung by the Cupid's arrow, she was stung by a repulsive arrow. Though not very common in love, this happens not infrequently.

Hooghly:	The Ganges is known by this name in Kolkata. Unlike the Brahmani, the Hooghly overflows throughout the year.
Jina:	The winner of hearts. She is beautiful, vivacious and to an extent boastful because of her beauty.
Jyoti:	Ordinarily means brilliance. Love infuses brilliance in a lover's eyes, so much so that he/she can see things with eyes closed.
Kalidas:	The court poet of King Vikramaditya. He had the blessings of Mother Saraswati and from a rustic youth he rose to become one of the most celebrated Sanskrit poets.
Konark:	The Sun Temple (also called the Black Pagoda). It is said that the magnificent temple was dashed to pieces in the wake of the curse of Chandrabhaga's sage father Sumanyu. What survives is the façade. However, the real cause of the collapse is a matter of conjecture.
Laxmi:	The Goddess of wealth. In a lover's heart the only wealth is the unending passionate thoughts that flow in from all sides.
Meghadoot:	One of Kalidas's immortal creations. Perhaps for the first time in literature the poet involved the Cloud as a messenger to carry the message of love from the lovelorn Yakshya to his consort.
Neelakantha (Das):	Odia poet and politician. A senior teacher of Satyabadi open air school, Neelakantha was an outstanding scholar.
Parijata:	The ever-fresh flower of the Nandan

	Kanan (Paradise). Sachi, Indra's queen, was fond of Parijata. Arguably, Parijata is the finest gift for a girl in love. That's why it finds frequent mention in love literature.
Puranic:	Relating to Indian scriptures.
Ramachandi:	The temple of Goddess Ramachandi is about three miles from Konark.
Sant Kabir:	A great mystic poet. According to him, love is the highest lesson in man's mundane existence. Love, he thought, was the only valuable lesson for a man to learn. Of course, love for him was love for God.
Smruti:	Memory, both sweet and bitter, with a clear tilt towards love.
Veena:	A variant spelling of Bina. But while Veena connotes a musical instrument, Bina brings to mind a beautiful girl with a musical temperament.
Yakshya:	An accursed demigod who was made to stay away from her consort for a year. In Kalidas's Meghadootam, the lovelorn Yakshya ventured to ask the cloud to carry his message to her pining consort.

BLACK EAGLE BOOKS

www.blackeaglebooks.org
info@blackeaglebooks.org

Black Eagle Books, an independent publisher, was founded as a nonprofit organization in April, 2019. It is our mission to connect and engage the Indian diaspora and the world at large with the best of works of world literature published on a collaborative platform, with special emphasis on foregrounding Contemporary Classics and New Writing.

www.ingramcontent.com/pod-product-compliance
Lightning Source LLC
Chambersburg PA
CBHW020541080526
44583CB00013B/931